MW01103590

To:

From:

The *Truth* About **MOM**

by Ben Mason

PORTLAND, OREGON

"Yes, Lord, I see that premarital sex probably wasn't the best choice."

"If I didn't know any better, I'd say that is a Slayer tattoo on the back of your neck."

"Easy there. You start off touching your toes — next thing you know you're blind by the time you're six."

"And this is where
Ted hid after his last
nervous breakdown."

"Hey! I told you kids to stop

looking at each other

like that."

"I attribute my atheism to my mother's bizarre role as the lone clergy member in what she called 'The Church of the Towels'."

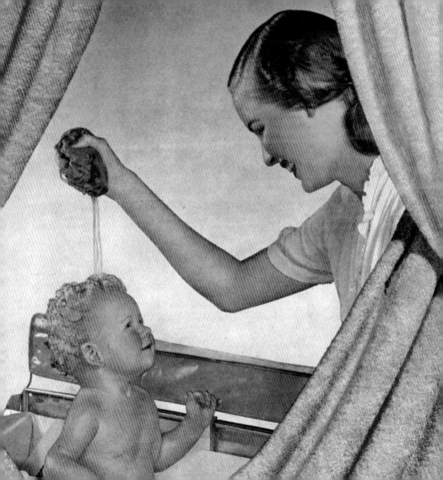

"Honey, how many times have I told you not to walk to work backwards? It confuses the children."

"Having my entire spinal column fused was rough at first, but maintaining perfect poise is worth it."

Even Dr. Freud was stumped when asked to help Linda sort out her relationship with her son.

"Making a home facial

is a real bitch."

"No, no, baby. It's no more breasts for you! You'll just have to get by with the bottle, like Daddy."

23

"Just put it right there, honey, next to the pint of O Positive."

"No, sweetie. Don't be silly.

You're not the evil one."

"So, Sally, I take it they haven't touched upon the concept of personal space in school yet, huh?"

"Heh-heh . . . you're so talented, Frannie. But let's not draw pictures of Mommy and Daddy 'loving each other' ever again, okay?"

31

Even on separate beds,
lavender sheets were the
height of risqué — and
were certainly never to
be seen by outsiders.

Phoebe impressed her family regularly with the muscle-toning properties of meat handling.

When guests were expected,
Mom took it upon herself
to inspect every square to
make sure it stuck to its
two-ply promise.

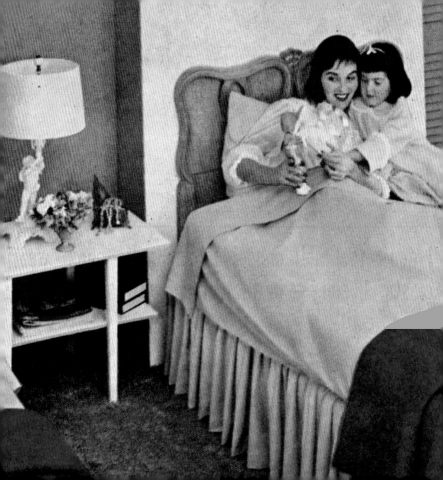

"Why is Mommy still in bed? Well, you see that needy, bratty look on Dolly's face . . . ?"

"We've timed it out perfectly: as soon as Junior finishes counting and sorting all the nuts, bolts, and washers in the bucket, we know it's time to dry the clothes!"

"Looks like baby inherited
Daddy's digestive tract!"

"Here, *you* ask Daddy what the parole board said."

Mom was color-blind and green was the cheapest, so she and Dad were both happy.

"Jeesh. I need to lay off
the starch next time."

"Holding the laundry after I've washed and folded it doesn't count as 'doing housework,' Ted."

"Wait, who the hell
is this one for?"

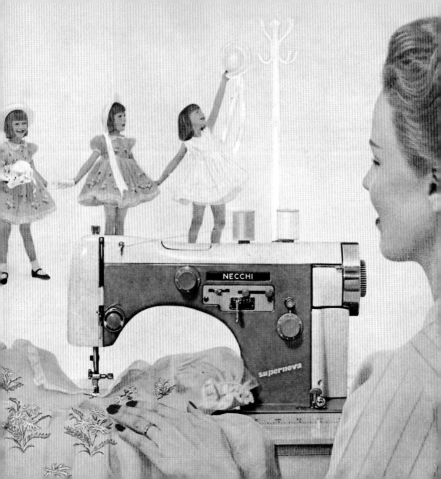

Mom's choice of the toyish
yellow color for the litter box
was perhaps not the best.

"The ladies' model even
comes with matching
metallic-blue earrings!"

Just one wash with
all-purpose Cheer and all
traces of the knife fight
were gone.

"See? It comes with the first piece already missing. That way, Frank thinks someone has beaten him to it, he gets demoralized, and then he gives up."

Back then, the side effects of amphetamine, or "mother's little helper," were not widely understood.

"Hey, *I* made the damn things!"

"I don't care what your little friend's mom says; Jesus would've broken enriched bread if he'd had the choice!"

"Lick the spoon?

Don't be silly, honey.

This is fruitcake batter."

It seemed a simple gift, but Laverne's mother had NO idea what she was starting.

After only
200,000 glass lifts,
Mom's wrists were
finally as thin as
her waist.

"Then Vice President Johnson asked Mrs. Lincoln, 'Yeah, but how was the play?'"

Somehow Mom got the idea
that margarine would increase
our growth rate.

"I wonder if our poor,
young, tanned and brawny
pool cleaner could help
me out with some of
these dishes . . . "

Mom was never subtle
when it came to making
her "I Feel So Trapped By
This Life" speech.

"Madge, I've told you we don't have time for this sort of thing anymore. The boy is blind — it's just cruel!"

"After Atkins, I'll be
able to wear this."

"And the magazines slip under there like so . . . "

"Feeding them once every two weeks makes them appreciate me that much more."

Bonnie tried to be stoic as the doctor broke the news of her latest pregnancy.

Miriam still marveled at
how much the baby resembled
her husband — a pure yet
fortuitous coincidence.

"The only drawback to our new zero-gravity kitchen is that I have to staple my skirt to my inner thighs."

95

More
Suburban
Confessions

BEN MASON has established himself as one of the most gifted semi-comedic writers to emerge from the southern southwest San Joaquin Valley, California (excluding Bakersfield, Taft, and Delano). His first novel, *Sunrise on Moonville*, was published in the spring of 2005, and he has also published fiction and poetry in *Calliope*, *Perigee*, and *Pacific Review*. Ben resides in Portland, Oregon.

Design: Kevin A. Welsch, Collectors Press, Inc. | Editor: Jade Chan

Printed in China
9 8 7 6 5 4 3 2 1

Library of Congress Cataloging-in-Publication Data

Mason, Ben, 1975-
 Suburban confessions : the truth about mom / Ben Mason.-- 1st American ed.
    p.   cm.
 ISBN 1-933112-10-7 (hardcover : alk. paper)
 1. Mothers--Humor. I. Title.
 PN6231.M68M37 2005
 818'.602--dc22
                                   2005011995

For a free catalog or special sales:
Collectors Press, Inc., P.O. Box 230986, Portland, OR 97281.
Toll-free: 1-800-423-1848 or visit collectorspress.com.